Cate Hollis and Mark Wheeller

Kindness: A Legacy of the Holocaust

A verbatim play based on the testimony of Holocaust survivor Susan Pollack MBE, with additional material by Cate Hollis and Voices of the Holocaust

Commissioned by Voices of the Holocaust

Salamander Street

PLAYS

First published in 2021 by Salamander Street Ltd.
(info@salamanderstreet.com)

Kindness: A Legacy of the Holocaust © Cate Hollis and Mark Wheeller, 2021

Reprinted with revisions in 2021.

ISBN: 9781914228186

10 9 8 7 6 5 4 3 2

CONTENTS

Acknowledgements

Susan Pollack MBE for her words and permission to use her emotive story.

Voices of the Holocaust who provided the opportunity and inspiration to create this important play.

Susan and Abraham Pollack, Professor Bob Skloot, Professor Belarie Zatzman, Michael Berenbaum, Rachel Century, Arnold Mittelman, Reverend Liz Baker, Julia Simmons – Collar.

All those whose testimonies and experiences are represented in this play. May their memories be a blessing.

The cast who performed a privately arranged staged reading of the play at the King Alfred Phoenix Theatre – Lawrence Stubbings, Nathaniel Thomas, Pamela Kay and Christianne Doran – and the 'Voices' family, especially Leona Day and Joanne Mulley.

Transcriptions of the testimony predominantly by Joanne Mulley.

George Spender from Salamander Street for his belief in our work.

Sophie Gorell Barnes and all at MBA for their continued support.

Neil, Nicholas and the rest of my (Cate's) family for their unwavering support in this play and the Voices' mission.

Rachel, and my (Mark's) family, who encourage my commitment to writing these plays.

Introduction by Cate Hollis

"Do we not know more about the War of the Roses and history of Britain from Shakespeare than from Holinshed's chronicles? If ever the past needs a human shape, it is the Holocaust" *(Daniel R. Schwarz)*.

Edward Bond, in his writings, takes the stance that imagination should be at the heart of all education, including and especially in the subject of the Holocaust, because the imagination is our humanity, the loss of which leaves humans as a product and sets us on the road to Auschwitz. He makes this dehumanisation the subject of his 2007 play *Coffee*; an examination of the Einsatzgruppen mass murders at Babi Yar.

In *Moral Dilemmas* Holocaust educator Paul Salmons states that "once the Holocaust is understood as a human event, it is perhaps inevitable that we reflect upon what this tells us about humanity". It then surely follows that drama and theatre, subjects fundamentally rooted in humanity and imagination, are the obvious tools for addressing these issues. If we use artistic means to shape – not to 'make up truths' but to make sense of existent ones – and use theatrical form to help process difficult knowledge in an "intertwining between thinking and imagination" then in so doing, we are able to imagine in order to look forward into our own lives and world.

In his first collection of Holocaust plays, Professor Robert Skloot discusses the way every 'significant human event' causes "nations and people to rethink the central questions of existence... as history is retold and re-experienced in song and story, poem and play... it has forced individuals to reassess their knowledge of the human species."

We sadly now face a period where living memory is increasingly moving into history. As we lose our survivors' voices in classrooms, so theatre can step in as a surrogate human voice. The Holocaust literature scholar Lawrence Langer often discusses the need to tread carefully in relation to theatrical structures. The word 'theatrical' is an unfortunate one for us. We must always avoid the histrionics or melodrama of the wrong kind of 'theatrical' – those that lead to the teenagers 'screaming to death in a gas chamber' on stage in an effort to gain an A grade. But, to allow the voices and the narrative to speak for themselves and to find meaningful form to do so is the key. In the work of *Voices of the Holocaust*, we propose that for a sound pedagogical approach to Holocaust education through theatre, the following issues need consideration;

- **The authentic voice and creating a landscape of culture and Judaism**; to counter the attempted annihilation of real lives, culture and faith in its entirety.

- **Representation**; the nature and complexity of what and how that process was undertaken, and the use of considered, sensitive and appropriate artistic form to do so.

- **Presenting context and complexity**; not a simplified and reductive approach (as Sir Ken Robinson discussed in his 'fast food' versus organic education TED talks). This includes an understanding that redemptive endings and messages cannot be imposed in places where they are not.

- **The importance of time for reflection**; whether through workshop / further classroom practice. Even in a staging of this play, students must be afforded the time to consider and process difficult understandings of the nature of society, humanity and the historic conditions that allowed the Holocaust to happen.

It has been an honour over the years to meet and work with survivors, both of the Holocaust and of subsequent genocides – from Rwanda, Darfur, Bosnia and Cambodia. The truth is that whilst the Holocaust was the first industrialised mass murder of its kind and on a scale so enormous many will never be able to comprehend, it was not the last genocide. The questions I am so often asked are "how do you deal with that?" or "what do we learn from that?" It's a very complex and personal question. One of my student's responses some time ago was "that human beings suck". My response was "but human beings can also be magnificent". Which is why it was important to include in *Kindness* the true story of Mala and Edek as well as a mention of Father Maximilian Kolbe; balance and counterbalance are essential.

Bringing Mark on board was so important in the creation of *Kindness*. As the country's most prolific and widely studied verbatim playwright, who better to take the testimony of Susan and to structure and shape her story from that time into an accessible piece of theatre? My role in the team became primarily the creation of the imaginative additions and the complementary narratives; to walk the pedagogical line and give teachers the springboards into historic, religious, SMSC ideas / understandings and the metaphorical layers, imagery and themes.

My hope is that both Drama teachers and teachers of History, RE, SMSC and their students, will find in this play a thought provoking narrative and characters through whom they can find questions for themselves, if not answers. I hope it will offer starting points for further learning and into sharing Susan's life experience far and wide. I am honoured to call Susan a friend, and I hope that this play will be embraced; to ensure that her experiences and those of her family and the other characters within will provide purpose and meaning for a long time to come.

For further guidelines on Holocaust education in Drama, please see the excellent guide created by the Holocaust Education Trust and teaching resources from the Holocaust Memorial Day Trust. For additional resources to support teaching Kindness *please contact VoicesoftheHolocaust.org.uk.*

Cate Hollis Biography

After twenty years as a Head of Drama, advisor and examiner, Cate left full time teaching to found *Voices of the Holocaust*. As the only specialist Holocaust theatre in education company, grounded in years of research and the collective informed advice and wisdom of educators and academics from all over the world, *Voices* has toured the UK, performed at the European Parliament and received standing ovations at the International Jewish Theatre Awards. Cate has been nominated for Pride of Britain, National Diversity and NICE *(excellence in cultural innovation)* awards.

Voices began with the original play *Butterflies* devised / written by Cate and a dedicated team of young actors which was based on the story of Hana Brady, first explored by Cate at a National Drama conference with renowned Professor Belarie Zatzman from Toronto University. It led to further study, a number of postgraduate qualifications including a Masters from Warwick University and meeting numerous inspirational survivors and educators who persuaded Cate to change direction and dedicate her professional life to telling the stories that needed to be told.

Cate lives in Milton Keynes with her very patient partner, a usually patient seven-year-old and an impatient house bunny who has a tendency to chew through her laptop cable and slow her down when she is working from home. In her spare time she volunteers at a homeless shelter when she is not cooking in her kitchen or becoming something of an expert in space and dinosaurs thanks to a small boy. In the year of Covid, Cate has been loving working as a support worker for adults with learning disabilities.

Introduction by Mark Wheeller

I had just completed the (then) new edit of *Too Much Punch For Judy* (25th anniversary production) when I had an email from Cate (Hollis) asking if I would be interested in a commission to jointly write a (verbatim) play for her company, Voices of the Holocaust.

"The play should tell, in a sensitive but dynamic and engaging verbatim approach, the history of the Holocaust through the eyes of the survivor*(s)* whose narratives we choose to work with. It needs to incorporate pre-war Jewish life and the implications of survival or otherwise."

What an opportunity!

I had known Cate for a short while, having met her at a National Drama conference. We were introduced to each other as she was (then) the Head of Drama at my beloved Stantonbury Campus. Shortly after this, I supported her as she put on an accomplished production of *Hard To Swallow* with her students. I was so proud to have my production performed in the theatre that had inspired my work so many years previously.

I was somewhat overawed by the subject matter of the proposed commission. I knew nothing more about it than the basic headline information. I felt it might be out of my depth but Cate reassured me, saying that I could rely on her expertise… as indeed was the case.

I felt I shouldn't be totally unprepared so I went to a bookshop to buy a book on the Holocaust. I selected *Auschwitz* by Laurence Rees and I remember being relieved to hear from Cate that this was perhaps the best choice… why didn't I ask her initially?

I was concerned the book was l o n g and feared it would be too academic for little old me and I wouldn't understand it. History at school had put me off such tomes!

As I read it, I remember thinking how history is mis-sold in schools as this dusty, academic subject. The Holocaust was simply a story… a horrific and appalling story but eminently readable… and, like other plays I'd worked on, told of people thrown into an exceptional situation. It had happened… actually happened to these real people. It was totally authentic. For the first time I regretted being put off history at school with its cloak of academia, making it appear distant and therefore not about real people like you and me.

The authenticity was something we were keen to capture in the play. Cate had the contacts and soon we were travelling to interview Susan Pollack MBE, a Holocaust survivor. I had never imagined the honour of sitting in the same room as someone who had had to endure this horror let alone being permitted to ask her questions about it.

Cate offered to run the interview for me but I was keen to take this on saying something to the effect of: "I need to ask all the naive questions as that is the position our audience will be in." As I said it, I realised that this was what I'd always done. I had never pre-researched the stories I told. There was often no way of doing this. I went in knowing nothing but needing to know everything… everything… no assumptions whatsoever. Cate was able to add to the process considerably by asking questions to highlight something I wouldn't know needed to be included so this two pronged approach added to the 'story' from a most willing Susan, keen to have her story out there as her legacy.

I remember one moment where the situation transcended academic history as she described arriving at Auschwitz and the tram door opening to reveal a good looking Nazi soldier. She said this with a smile.

I saw this, this… er… German guard… this… er… nice, handsome man. A soldier… well-dressed. Handsome, proud and cruel. But not smiling. He was ordering.

It was such a 'real' reflection. There were so many more of these in the play. What Susan offered was an authentic reminiscence of something we simply have to know about. Her story is beyond important.

The Voices team took on the huge task of transcribing (complete with um's and er's) the complete testimony and soon I was able to use this to make the main body of the play. I used exclusively Susan's words to lay out her story allocating them to others she referred to.

I remember one idea I had was that gradually the other characters would disappear (as they tragically did) and would leave Susan alone on stage delivering a monologue. This didn't happen in the final versions of the play but the idea of being gradually and heartbreakingly isolated from those she loved is something I would like a director to consider when staging the play.

I was never asked to re-write any sections which gave me confidence particularly as I had started this project feeling overawed. This led me to realise I did have a 'method' for my verbatim projects – to go in with little research so that I can ask the naive questions. I often cite this play when people talk to me about my research 'methods'.

Just prior to the first UK lockdown (2020), Cate took a group from Voices to present a reading to Susan. Afterwards, she received this generous message from Susan:

I had the pleasure of listening to the replay of my Holocaust experience. I sincerely felt very moved and grateful that the play Kindness *so accurately represented my experiences, and that the mood and political situation of the time is so accurately shown.*

Thank you so much,

Susan Pollack.

I feel that this is one of the most important accounts that could ever be turned into a stage play and am supremely grateful to Cate for inviting me to be part of the team who put it together.

Thanks to my publisher Salamander Street, schools now have the opportunity to explore the play and a period of world history which is not just something to be studied in history books but a series of not to be forgotten personal stories.

Thank you Susan for your willingness to trust us both in this venture.

Mark Wheeller Biography

Mark Wheeller began writing whilst a student at Marlwood Comprehensive School, Bristol. After teaching drama for thirty-six years he retired in July 2015 to concentrate on writing and delivering Drama/Theatre workshops to students and teachers across the world.

Mark is one of the most-performed playwrights in Britain. *Too Much Punch For Judy* has been performed over 6,000 times and *Chicken!* nearly 6,000. *Missing Dan Nolan* and *Hard to Swallow* are both set texts for the GSCE Drama 9-1 exams. His work has been a staple part of the Drama curriculum both in the UK and abroad for the past three decades. Professional productions of *Hard to Swallow, I Love You, Mum – I Promise I Won't Die* and *Chicken!* regularly tour schools and many of Mark's works are available on DVD and digital formats. His study guides include *Drama Schemes, The Story Behind Too Much Punch For Judy, Drama Club* & *Hard to Swallow – Easy to Digest*. Salamander Street are pleased to be publishing a new career retrospective book Mark wrote during the lockdown, *Verbatim – The Fun Of Making Theatre Seriously*.

He has three children and lives just outside the New Forest, with his wife Rachel, and Labrador, Dusty.

A Note on Inverted Commas

When one approaches the language of the Holocaust, one has to appreciate that Nazi terminology amounted to a sort of Orwellian 'Newspeak'; that is to say a language used to deliberately deceive / conceal the reality of what the terminology was truly referring to. Thus, it is vital that when approaching terms like 'resettlement' *(forced removal to be murdered)*, 'special treatment' *(murder)*, 'euthanasia' *(murder)*, 'cleansing' *(mass murder)*, 'final solution' *(total annihilation)*, one must be aware of the true reality of this doublespeak and, in the case of an actor, make a decision on the use of that language according to its context. This is the language of a murderous, genocidal regime and its euphemisms must be approached with an understanding of its offences.

A Note on Stone Setting

Stone settings are an ancient tradition in Jewish culture. Rather than laying flowers on a grave, it is instead traditional to place a stone. The origins of this tradition are unclear, but the permanence of the stone is a means of honouring the dead. It symbolises a legacy / bond and marks the memory of the loved one at the grave. It is worth noting that many Holocaust memorials around the world are rooted in this tradition and are thought provoking artistic reflections on the Shoah in addition to their role to memorialise.

A Note on Humanity

To dehumanise was a fundamental principle of the regime that conducted the Holocaust. In their language, their propaganda, their systematic removal of dignity, identity, community, nationality, culture, faith and ultimately life, the Nazi regime attempted to dismantle humanity. There are many stories – told and untold – of those who refused to allow that to happen. They are crucial and must continue to be told.

In *Kindness*, it is the responsibility of those telling these stories to hold that critical humanity at the heart of their narrative journey. To shock, to debase and reduce victims of the Holocaust to that which the Nazis attempted to turn them into is to remove their dignity yet again. Give every individual their real identity and their true value and speak for the survivors and victims. For this reason, *Kindness* is steeped in Jewish music and culture. In its use of projected images, it reflects on lives as they were lived. Its stories of resistance, struggle and survival remind us that whilst the fragility of humanity can be bewildering, the possibilities of the human spirit are remarkable.

In bequeathing the story of this period of her life to us, Susan is entrusting us with her testimony and it is our crucial responsibility to ensure that we bear witness and re-humanise those who were robbed of it.

Characters

RABBI

SUSAN

LACI

MOTHER

FATHER

MRS SCHWARTZ

CHRISTIAN WOMAN

GENDARME

KAPO

GERMAN SOLDIER

MALA

EDEK

SURVIVOR 1

SURVIVOR 2

SURVIVOR 3

WOMAN 1

WOMAN 2

MAN 1

MAN 2

BRITISH SOLDIER

LACI'S WIFE

SUGGESTED CHARACTER SPLIT FOR FOUR ACTORS:

ACTOR 1

SUSAN, WOMAN 2

ACTOR 2

MOTHER, MALA, MRS SCHWARTZ, LACI'S WIFE, WOMAN 1, SURVIVOR 3

ACTOR 3

LACI, RABBI, MAN 1, SURVIVOR 2

ACTOR 4

FATHER, EDEK, GERMAN SOLDIER, BRITISH SOLDIER, MAN 2, SURVIVOR 1

All other parts to be split as is practical.

Preset: A bare tree (the tree of life) stands CSR. Beneath it a pile of stones, added to at key moments during the course of the play (see notes). Empty picture frames suspended from the branches, with the exception of the photograph of **SUSAN** *as a girl prior to the Holocaust, lit at key moments.*

SL in front of a partial wall onto which images / film are projected is a pile of suitcases, spilling out a mound of abandoned detritus of lives as lived; an old telephone, clothes, shoes, prayer books, Shabbat candlesticks, a sewing machine etc.

SR is a wooden cart, a metal bath tub, a sewing machine and bundles.

Three tall wooden A frame ladders mark the perimeter of the rest of the playing space and function to provide playing levels for the actors, for suspending the swastica banners and so forth during the course of the action. Costume items for the actors as they role change are part of the piles of abandoned belongings of a community destroyed by the atrocities of the Holocaust across Europe. The actors begin dressed in grey – a blank canvas.

Section 1

PROLOGUE

Blackout. Hine Ma Tov – sung or played quietly – opens the play.

RABBI: As Mala Zimetbaum and Edek Galinski sat in their separate cells awaiting their executions, both knew they had each others' hearts and no matter how terrifying the journey would be to their deaths, they would always be alive in the other's hopes and dreams.

Cielito Lindo plays in the background.

After roll call each night the courtyard of the notorious Block 11 would be quiet but for a love song from Mexico. Each night, knowing that his lover Mala could hear him, Edek would sing to her. His voice as beautiful as her spirit.

It is said in Jewish culture that birds are a symbol of the soul. Many stories exist of how Mala finally met her end but some would have it that her spirit flew high, undefeated by the inhumanity of that dreadful place.

Music builds as the scene dissolves.

Section 2

FAMILY

SUSAN: I was born in 1930. My Hungarian name is Zsuzsanna. Blau was my maiden name. We hadn't Hungarianised it.

I hope this play will provide a permanent record. It stands as a… as a er… as a warning sign… against… not just against antisemitism but against any form of racism… and also to show that it can happen in a "civilized" country like Germany.

I am Susan Pollack.

LACI: Most Jews wanted, to kind of… to melt into the wider community.

MOTHER: There was always, you know, antisemitism in Hungary.

SUSAN: I hadn't suffered from it too much.

FATHER: We lived in Felsögod, a pretty village on the Danube. There were about eighteen Jewish families.

MOTHER: After our marriage we came to open up a small business selling wood and coal.

FATHER: We had this little house built with a big yard, and a few horses that helped us deliver the wood and coal.

SUSAN: *(Family image projected onto the SL wall as* **SUSAN** *takes a picture frame from the tree.)* I got a picture actually, of Father, the only one I have of my family. My brother, Laszlo – Laci, as we called him – was two years older.

LACI: I didn't have much time for Susan.

SUSAN: Once his friend brought along a camera so I kind of posed, and he said:

LACI: "You look like you're pregnant."

SUSAN: I've never forgotten that.

LACI: We were helpful, in the economy of the household.

SUSAN: I learnt to sew very early in my life er, which I enjoy doing even today.

LACI: We were expected to do things, serving customers, stacking the wood…

SUSAN: Looking after the geese and chickens, and in the house; cleaning, cooking, baking the bread.

LACI: We lived a lifestyle very close to the earth.

SUSAN: It was an enjoyable life, but I remember freezing cold winters…

LACI: Our dog, living outdoors, shivering away. And a cat too.

SUSAN: I wanted to rescue the poor things. My father… I remember him picking the cat up and throwing it out. I would not say anything.

LACI: He was the authority.

FATHER: A tall, handsome looking man. Very intelligent.

MOTHER: Mother was a submissive village lady who depended on him.

SUSAN: My father instilled a sense of patriotism in our lives. He told stories about his involvement in the First World War.

FATHER: I was captured by the Russians and taken prisoner but I escaped when I heard prisoners had been forced to go down to the river to be killed there.

SUSAN: He got out on the top of a train through Omsk, Tomsk, Irkutsk, Vladivostok. I remember that sequence of names coz he said it several times.

FATHER: When I reached Hungary I kissed the soil in gratitude.

LACI: He often repeated that story to us.

SUSAN: He felt very Hungarian.

FATHER: A Hungarian patriot.

Czárdás music in the background. A dance begins – an echo of the past.

SUSAN: When there were the occasional outcries against the Jews… he'd say:

FATHER: They're just local thugs.

SUSAN: So… I felt both Hungarian and Jewish. I liked the Hungarian culture. I'd peek into the pubs near the market place … the singing and dancing with their big skirts. I had this national costume and loved it. To this day I like Hungarian music.

LACI: It was a very simple… very simple, primitive lifestyle, but a meaningful life. It was a hard life, but we appreciated things.

SUSAN: I remember my friend's sister, she had a lovely skirt on and a beautiful blouse, and she was going to work in Budapest in an office. We admired her. She was just stepping out from this agrarian background into some sophisticated, elegant world.

LACI: Budapest was about forty-five minutes away by train but we were a world apart. We were cynical of their values and how they kept apart.

SUSAN: I went to a local school and learnt to read. I think I imagined just getting married young and having children. I wasn't entirely satisfied with that, but there was no way to escape.

LACI: As a Jewish family, we kept our festivals. And Shabbat.

The men begin humming 'Shalom Aleichem' and sequence of projected images of ordinary Jewish life in Hungary underscore.

SUSAN: There was always singing and always eating. My father was, I think, one of the organisers of the little synagogue in Felsögod… a sort of a wooden shack it was.

MOTHER: Sabbath was Holy.

SUSAN: We weren't even allowed to pick up a pencil.

MOTHER: Sabbath was for relaxation.

SUSAN: We had a bath before, on Friday. Food was cooked. Occasionally friends were invited. It was a day of… of peace, a day of holiness, a day of… of spirituality. It was a very welcome day… away from the harsh reality…

Section 3

THE TENSION INCREASES

FATHER: The harsh reality was always looming.

MOTHER: An indescribable feeling.

SUSAN: We were the outsiders.

FATHER: We prayed and felt; *(To the family.)* it will just blow over… will improve. This is just a temporary situation.

MOTHER: But desperation was always there.

FATHER: Politically it became more difficult. We had legislation from the Hungarian Government restricting Jewish boys and girls from going into further education.

SUSAN: This affected my brother who was a studious guy.

ALL: We lived in a total isolation.

Music and singing fades. Projection of images and film footage of book burnings, persecutions and other restrictions increasingly imposed by the Nazis in Germany and increasingly across Europe during Hitler's reign pre-war (1933 – 1939) underscore the next section.

LACI: There was no international news or, at least, we didn't know about it.

FATHER: It was 1939. Hitler had come to power in 1933.

SUSAN: The Holocaust didn't just happen overnight. There was violence against my brother when he went to the Boys Brigade.

MOTHER: They'd be waiting outside for him.

*Movement sequence as **LACI** is 'beaten up'; a stylised movement sequence. Short, but shocking.*

FATHER: Seventeen, eighteen year olds.

MOTHER: He managed to struggle home; limping, barely able to walk. He came home beaten up, black and blue… his face, his body. He was 11 years old.

LACI *returns; more a broken puppet than a person.*

SUSAN: The officials would just shrug their shoulders saying,

MEN: "They're just thugs, they're just irresponsible."

FATHER: There was nothing I could do. I'd say, I'd say…

SUSAN: He wouldn't actually say anything.

FATHER: I'd say: "I'll report it to the local council."

SUSAN: But there was no… no help.

LACI: Increasingly we'd have more graffiti on… on the wa-… on the street,

SUSAN: "Jews get out,"

LACI: "Go to Palestine."

SUSAN: We were held responsible for… the shortage of food…

LACI: Whatever problems they had; it was our fault.

SUSAN: Occasionally we were allowed to go to the cinema and saw Germans occupying different countries and the local population waving w-with joy at their… a-at their arrival.

ALL: Confusion set in our minds.

MOTHER: Didn't know which way to turn.

SUSAN: It was getting even more difficult:

LACI: The open violence…

FATHER: The graffiti…

SUSAN: And then… legislation in the early '40's.

LACI: Jews can't be civil servants anymore…

SUSAN: Lawyers were dismissed.

FATHER: Doctors can't practice.

MOTHER: The self-employed, like us, were shut down.

FATHER: We couldn't serve anybody…

MOTHER: …couldn't buy or sell…

FATHER: …or trade in any way.

MOTHER: It made us realise…

ALL: Something's looming.

> **FATHER** *begins work motif that becomes increasingly laboured.*

MOTHER: It was incomprehensible to our mind. We just couldn't understand it.

LACI: The only thing Father could find, to sustain the family to keep us, was manual work in a Budapest factory.

SUSAN: He became withdrawn and… wasn't approachable.

LACI: He had no answers.

MOTHER: He came home feeling very tired, you know, carrying heavy loads all day on his back…

> **FATHER** *returns, exhausted.*

LACI: Jews were dismissed from any kind of, any managerial post.

SUSAN: We kept to ourselves.

LACI: We wouldn't go out in the street on our own anymore.

MOTHER: We were fearful because violence was not only allowed, but promoted. There was nothing we could do… nothing… we were totally impotent.

LACI: The other persecutions were never on the newsreel so… we had no idea what was taking place elsewhere… that Jews had been transported.

SUSAN: We Jews remained in Hungary… the very last country to…

MOTHER: There was fear when you watched the Nazis marching.

FATHER: We saw… we saw the might of the German army.

MOTHER: It was a blind fear. Who could actually imagine? Who could have explained that human beings are capable of such atrocities? If someone had told us, I don't suppose we would have believed them.

Swastica banners are dropped from the top of the ladders, to hang prominently on display.

Section 4

SEGREGATION

SUSAN: We believed it would blow over.

ALL: We prayed.

LACI: We turned to religion.

> **FATHER** and **LACI** *pray.* **SUSAN** *collects the sewing machine and stars / additional costume items with stars attached.*

MOTHER: We had to wear yellow stars… all Jews… irrespective of age, had to wear a yellow star of a certain size to be identified.

SUSAN: The Hungarian gendarmes came to the house telling us what to do saying:

GENDARMES: That is our order. That's what you need to do… NOW.

MOTHER: They… they arrived, brought the cloth…

SUSAN: And we sewed it up.

MOTHER: We did everything we were asked.

FATHER: Identification with the yellow star allowed us to use the trains.

LACI: My father was looking for a secondary school for Susan. It was difficult.

SUSAN: Finally he found one. We were segregated. There were maybe ten Jewish students, sitting at the back, with two empty rows between us and the rest of the class. Outside in the playground, we were segregated from the other children so that um, so um, that shadowy reality became quite, quite clear in my head.

LACI: Communication between us and the rest of the class was forbidden.

SUSAN: We became silent. We knew that there was a hatred against the Jews, but we had no information whatsoever what the end product of… of… of all this persecution will be… "The Blaming of the Jews" as it was called.

SUSAN & LACI: In 1943 the school was closed down.

MRS SCHWARTZ: Young Jews were being arrested.

LACI: The Hungarian Gendarmes didn't have any reasons… they just arrested…

FATHER: They took boys and children off the streets and we haven't seen them since.

MRS SCHWARTZ: My children. My children didn't come home.

SUSAN: They'd been identified by the yellow stars.

FATHER: We had no idea where they had gone.

SUSAN: There were rumours…

LACI: Rumours about this "resettlement programme"…

SUSAN: That eventually you'd be taken, you know, from your home, and resettled somewhere in the east. That was about all. The whole… the whole village changed their behaviour towards us, very quickly.

MOTHER: Neighbours kept to the other side of the road. Before, you know, we'd chatter, on the street… you know, discussing the children, how mothers do.

SUSAN: Now they avoided us.

MOTHER: Propaganda pervaded their minds, completely, from church, from… from politics. *We* were the pariah…

SUSAN: There were some, I heard afterwards, who offered rescue places, but that didn't happen to us.

MOTHER: We, we were afraid, to approach them, because we didn't know who is a Nazi, who is a fascist.

LACI: They were grey days… very dismal.

SUSAN: Somehow… the sun… The sun just went to sleep.

LACI: My parents felt, you know, as law-abiding citizens they should follow the legislations but, on the other hand, we felt that violence could break out and hurt us so we kept qu-… very quiet.

FATHER: Nothing was discussed.

SUSAN: If you have no options, no solutions, and not even a glimpse of hope, what can you share?

FATHER: Silence, disbelief and shrugging.

LACI: The biggest problem we had was the lack of any information.

MOTHER: All we could hope for, was that the Russians would come soon.

Section 5

THE MEN ARE TAKEN

SUSAN: In 1943 the hearsay of being transported became a reality.

MOTHER: The gendarmes came to our house. I told my husband what they said.

GENDARME: This gossip about the resettlements will be discussed at the town hall. You should attend. It's in your interest to come to discuss this resettlement programme.

MOTHER: So, he went with a few Jews who lived near us.

SUSAN: I think it was evening, yes, towards the evening. My mother probably was saying in a reassuring voice,

MOTHER: It… it's alright, your father knows what he's doing, he's very capable and, and have no fears.

SUSAN: She must have been extremely fearful and frightened. We walked through the street just, sort of, hanging on to my mother's clothes, and um, walking behind her – she was leading the way, through the market place, the market place, where I'd listened to the music. People were just going on as normal. Although it was dark we could see father.

MOTHER: We wanted to talk to him but we couldn't.

LACI: There were… maybe fifteen men and a truck waiting.

MOTHER: We were kept away. There was this… this… terror…

SUSAN: Our men were being brutally beaten up and herded onto this truck. We were absolutely terrified.

MOTHER: They'd expected a discussion… not…

LACI: … not transportation.

SUSAN: No one explained anything.

LACI: No one apologised.

MOTHER: Nothing.

SUSAN: It was torment.

LACI: It was a show of power to warn us.

MOTHER: Then they were driven off.

SUSAN: We walked back in silence. I haven't seen him since. My mother might have said:

MOTHER: Oh, we'll see him soon.

SUSAN: But I doubted I would. We found out where they were taken to, but by then it was forbidden to use the public transport so uh, we…

MOTHER: We managed, to… to pay a local lady… a Christian lady, who we gave a basket of food to take to him.

SUSAN: She came back with information:

WOMAN: Mrs Blau, just as well you haven't seen your husband.

LACI: He had been brutally treated. 'Unrecognisable' was what she said.

SUSAN: I have no idea whether he died in Hungary, in that camp, or whether he was transported to another. So, that… that was that. That was the… the disappearance of the men, from all the provincial villages and towns.

(The family place stones at the foot of the tree; a motif to be echoed through the rest of the play.)

FATHER: The rest of the family were taken in May or June 1944…

Section 6

RESETTLEMENT

SUSAN: Five or six months after father was taken and a month before Mala Zimetbaum and Edek Galinski escaped Auschwitz – Birkenau – Eichmann, the notorious Nazi – one of the curators of the Holocaust – came to Hungary with a small occupation army because the Hungarians were collaborators.

LACI: The Gendarmes came to our door again:

GENDARME: You know of the resettlement program. You be ready in the morning.

SUSAN: We stayed up all night… started baking… I think we cooked some, uh, I don't know, some, some, potatoes we found in the cellar perhaps.

LACI: Mother got hold of some meat that wasn't kosher and fed it to us.

SUSAN: Ironically it was the end of May 1944 and it was Shavuot.

MOTHER: *(Regretfully.)* No dairy.

SUSAN: She wouldn't let us in the house with it… we had to eat outside, you know. We were glad to have it…

MOTHER: It was good food. *(With great sadness.* **MOTHER** *begins to collect together bundles and gives each child something to carry in addition to taking something herself.)*

LACI: It must have been very hard for her but she gave it to us to give us strength. We had no real luggage… that was a luxury we couldn't afford. So we took a sheet, put it on our backs, and put the food and a few bits of clothes in it.

SUSAN: I carried a, a sewing machine, believe it or not. I carried a sewing machine! I was thirteen. I could operate it and my mum, I think my mother must have said…

MOTHER: This resettlement, wherever we are, at least we've got a little bit of skill.

They leave, waiting for **SUSAN**, *who takes a moment to reflect before joining them.*

SUSAN: I took a little handkerchief that had some small pieces of uh, of broken gold jewellery that I used to look at as a little child, knowing they were precious, so it was something I enjoyed looking at.

MOTHER: We were taken at six, by train, to Vac…

They move onto the train – a motif to be replicated later.

SUSAN: … where I went to that school…

LACI: It was set up as a ghetto.

SUSAN: Not ghettos like the ones in countries like Poland that were shown in many films years later.

LACI: The windows were blackened and there were bunk-beds in the classrooms.

They gather in a huddle SR on the edge of the tipped up cart.

MOTHER: We ate the food we had brought with us.

SUSAN: I threw that little handkerchief with the bits and pieces away because of the propaganda…

LACI: *(Sarcastically.)* "Jews are hoarders of gold"….

SUSAN: We didn't want to be… we were frightened to be found with it.

LACI: There were about fifteen to twenty people.

SUSAN: All the beds were, sort of, next to each other. There were no men, of course, because the men were all taken… only women, children and elderly people. I can remember people saying:

ALL: Dear G-d, help us. Help us, help us.

MOTHER: There was no… no energy left to raise any voices against, and… well…Oy vey! We were fearful that had we done that, we'd receive, er, physical punishment.

SUSAN: We were not allowed out of the ghetto – the school. Not given anything… no food… we were desperately hungry, just looking for crumbs.

LACI: The horror was…

MOTHER: It made us absolutely numb.

SUSAN: Laci was um, just deprived, totally, of… of any masculine retaliation… because, I mean, we had no guns…and if we had, how can you… what can you do? There was just nothing that we could…

MOTHER: We were trapped.

LACI: The gendarmes were all around.

SUSAN: We'd go out to the toilet and see them but we didn't want to be seen.

MOTHER: Five days later we were taken away….

SUSAN: Nobody said where you were going, it was just –

ALL: "Get on!"

SUSAN: No instructions whatsoever just a long train journey…

MOTHER: To a disused mine…

LACI: With little huts at the side of the pit… a *huge* place…

SUSAN: The three of us – my mother, my brother and me – were still together and I'm still carrying my sewing machine. It was getting warmer.

LACI: It was a long walk from the train station to this mine…

MOTHER: Two or three hours.

SUSAN: And they'd shoot us if we tried to go somewhere.

MOTHER: There were hundreds in this internment camp. We had to sleep outdoors. *(Disbelief takes over from fear.)*

LACI: People from other villages, from other towns being gathered here.

SUSAN: It was the first time I'd seen so many people…

MOTHER & LACI: So many people. *(Despair takes over from disbelief.)*

LACI: And the Hungarian gendarmes watching us. You know, with guns, ready to shoot.

SUSAN: We were exhausted after the long walk and realised we were doomed. It's as simple as that; we were doomed…

MOTHER: No escape… never.

LACI: We had no food left.

SUSAN: *(To LACI.)* See that queue?

LACI: There were queues established, you know, to different sheds.

SUSAN: Maybe there's food, being distributed.

LACI: We stood there, but we never got any food.

SUSAN: We didn't even get close to it… and sometimes they'd say,

GENDARME: Pah! *(Contemptuously.)* If you'd converted to Christianity you might escape!

SUSAN: Which, of course, we know *now* would not have been possible even if we *had* been willing.

LACI: We didn't stay there long…

MOTHER: Three or four days in the heat…

LACI: With no food and no water. It's a long time… a long time.

SUSAN: We just sat and, and, and s-scrambled in the, in the dirt… just drawing with a… a broken branch ju-just, in a stupor. Mother was, was absolutely destroyed…

LACI: Totally destroyed… you could see it on her face.

SUSAN: There were toilets there, open latrines, very deep… with a plank of wood going across, you know, for sitting down, and, er, little children fell into it. There were no implements so we couldn't rescue them. I saw them… you could see them at the bottom. *(Stones placed by other actors as SUSAN speaks.)* You can imagine how demoralised we felt and… and there was no… no drinking water.

Section 7

THE CATTLE WAGON

MOTHER: After three or four days we were told to start walking for a good few hours… Several hours after three days of just morsels of food… leftovers.

SUSAN: We could see in the distance a long train… a cattle train.

LACI: It was obviously waiting for us.

SUSAN: We'd given up asking questions.

MOTHER: We walked there, towards the train.

SUSAN: I had lost my sewing machine…. it was taken… I don't know where.

LACI: People still had bags or sheets with far less belongings than they originally had. *(Clutches his bundle tightly.)* they'd got more tired.

MOTHER: The food was long since gone.

SUSAN: The train doors were opened.

LACI: There was straw on the bottom.

MOTHER: Small windows right at the top, with little, tiny little openings.

LACI: It was hot. Horribly hot.

SUSAN: There were about eighty of us. In others, as many as 150 crammed inside these wagons designed to take cattle to their slaughter. I later found out the longest transport was from Corfu – eighteen days. When they opened the doors, *everyone* was dead.

LACI: They put in two buckets… one drinking water, and the other one, you know…

SUSAN: The toilet was, er… nobody bothered using the bucket. We were sitting… you know… all crunched in, on top of each other. The doors were shut.

LACI: We were trapped.

SUSAN: We felt we were gonners… we were just…

ALL THREE: … just ghosts…

MOTHER: On a ghost train.

LACI: A journey to nowhere. We were suffocating.

MOTHER: Babies died.

LACI: Elderly died.

SUSAN: I was sitting next to my mother and brother. We never spoke… just sat in total disbelief… no comprehension just another… place of horror. The over-crowdedness was… was un-unspeakable… no air to breathe and little water. For days. I don't know how many… four maybe six days. The atmosphere was total despair. We knew we were being just annihilated. I can actually remember thinking that – vividly. It hasn't got that, sort of sharp edge anymore. It's numbed, but the… the pain is there, and that… that feeling of huge depression that completely overwhelms you is … part of that is still there. No one should ever have to try to imagine.

LACI: The train was jolting back and forth just to be cruel… you know… a few yards. There was no… no purpose to it.

MOTHER: The buckets were tipping…

LACI: … spilling all over the place.

SUSAN: There was a stench… you know… eighty people for all that time, and no toilets? These trains were… eh… for animals, so whenever it stopped people were shrieking out –

ALL: Please, please, give us some water.

MOTHER: People took turns in climbing up to the tiny little windows once in a while; stood on someone else to lift them up.

LACI: A look-out saw the name.

ALL: 'Auschwitz'.

MOTHER: It meant nothing.

Section 8

ARRIVAL AT AUSCHWITZ

SUSAN: When the doors opened up – such a relief.

ALL THREE: Fresh air.

SUSAN: I saw this, this… er… German guard… this… er… nice, handsome man. A soldier… well-dressed. Handsome, proud and cruel. But not smiling. He was ordering. You know, strong voice…

SOLDIER: Quick, quick! Very quick. Move!

SUSAN: In German…

SOLDIER: Raus! Raus!

SUSAN: We were… we were kind of glad – finally fresh air hit us.

MOTHER: It was the evening, so it was cool.

LACI: Those that could move, moved.

MOTHER: Many had died… just left there. Immediately the terror. The terror got into our bodies.

LACI: We got on the ramp, a concrete base about the size of a quarter of a football pitch… with a few uniformed Nazis… like we'd seen in the cinema. And some… some kapos…

MOTHER: Kapos were prisoners who were kind of bosses of the barracks… and in return they got more food.

SUSAN: One came past me and whispered:

KAPO: Don't say you're younger than fifteen. Say you're older.

SUSAN: He wasn't supposed to. He could have been shot.

LACI: There must have been one or two thousand on this ramp.

SUSAN: It was death… all around.

The platform at Auschwitz. Physical theatre sequence encapsulating the panic and fear – perhaps a dance echoing the Czárdás dancing from the pub in Felsögod in years gone by – interspersed with the monologues of other survivors.

SUSAN: Mother was taken away. It was very quick. There was no time to say goodbye. Nothing. No emotional kind of response to that. No time even to consider what was taking place. So you just follow orders. Just follow the others. "Go there. Go there. You, go here". My brother was also taken away. I can't imagine how I felt, the lack of food and lack of water, being separated in the middle of somewhere I don't know, with people I don't know. How on earth would you feel?

SURVIVOR 1: The sky was hazy and there was a terrible smell. From a distance we saw chimneys with smoke coming out. At the time we didn't realise what it was. But rumours started spreading that it was a crematorium. I still didn't know what that meant. We had to line up in front of the Nazis for 'selection'. As far as I know we were the only transport from the Łódź ghetto that arrived in Auschwitz with over 500 people who were all on a named list. We were confused. Terrified.

SURVIVOR 2: There were officers and men with guns standing by. There was panic all around us. Fear in everyone's eyes. They told all of us 185 children to walk with the other people to the left. Then they wanted a young woman who had her baby in her arms and they tried to take it out of her hands and she was screaming and screaming. The SS men ran towards her. Myself and another boy saw that the fitter people were being sent to the right so in the chaos we swapped sides. If we had not, in less than hour we would have been smoke and dust.

SURVIVOR 3: I came in the middle of the night. The whole place was lit up and there was kind of, like a smell of roasting meat. And you thought, G-d, surely they can't be roasting a load of meat here. And there was this kind of glow in the distance. And you thought – what on earth is this glow? We did not know where we were except for the stench. And the people came in the trains amongst the panic and the chaos. Just imagine, hundreds, thousands walking along this road with their bundles. Tiny children, old people. And they had to walk all the way to their end.

Section 9

DEHUMANISATION

SUSAN: You could feel the… feel the pain and despair and that oh… helplessness, again… I keep saying it… utter helplessness. Then the German… I think it was the notorious Dr Mengele, I don't know, came to me.

SOLDIER: Wie alt bist du?

SUSAN: Ich bin fifteen. I was reasonably tall for my age and he said in German:

SOLDIER: OK, you stay here.

SUSAN: If I'd said I was thirteen I'd've been sent to the gas chamber. One girl I had been with at some point said:

"Where's your mum?"

But she was selected when we arrived and put in another group with young children and babies. She was gassed.

LACI: Queues were formed.

SUSAN: Then… then you enter some world that is indes-, in-, indescribable. You're frozen… absolutely frozen… literally, you're frozen in fear. Your emotional life is… is… is no longer functioning, and unconsciously you don't allow that to enter into you because you could die in that minute… so… you're… you're just… you become a robot. I just followed the other girls. I think, being part of that little group I felt maybe… maybe we'd been er… we'd been chosen for something.

Our clothes were stripped and hair everywhere on the body was shaven off. Pink disinfectant was thrown on our body. We were told to pick up clothes and shoes from a mountain of clothes. There was no time to check,

"Is that my size?"

I picked up a small pair – I still have deformed toes.

They put us all into a big barrack… about a thousand girls. We slept, on big bunk beds… eight or ten on each level… one blanket between us. That was *our* existence in Auschwitz – to wait. We did nothing. We waited for food, which was very, very limited. A 'coffee' was all we got in the morning. In the evening we got so-called 'soup' with n-no nutritious content.

I didn't cry. All natural flow of humanity, feelings of knowing what this world is about and how to live our lives disappeared. I'd entered a world that was inconceivably strange, frightening and fearful. There was nothing to judge it by. I learnt very quickly that the way to survive was not to be noticed, and I soon realised that my clothes would have been from those sent to the gas chambers.

I don't remember the others' names in the barracks. Keeping relations needed energy, and we did not have that.

Survival wasn't just about the body, but also the soul. Keeping our imaginations alive was as important as our bodies.

Section 10

BODY AND SOUL

Music. The scene shifts. Two separate spots on stage – the two women in one space, the two men back to back in the other. The men quietly sipping their bowls of soup during the women's scene.

WOMAN 1: Let us prepare a feast! A feast like no other!

WOMAN 2: *(With effort.)* A *table* piled high with challah!

WOMAN 1: Cheeses! Juicy ripe fruits!

WOMAN 2: *(Gradually warming to the game.)* Gefilte fish! Latkes! Matzah balls in thick chicken soup!!

WOMAN 1: *(Encouraging.)* Yes!!!

WOMAN 2: Lokshen kugel! *(Exhausted, starving or perhaps overwhelmed by the fantasy, she groans.)*

WOMAN 1: *(Matter of fact / sternly.)* Girl. You survive. You have to. For all your family who they sent through the chimney. *You survive* – physically *and* mentally. *Take from the dead* – if you don't, someone else will. Their possessions are no use to them when they are gone. And here. *(Pulls a strand of wool from a tired looking shawl wrapped around her shoulders.)* Tie that bowl to your waist. Someone takes that off you in the night you'll have nothing to eat from and you'll be dead soon enough. *(Pause.)* And sharpen up for roll call. Get some colour in your cheeks however you can. Mostly they prick their fingers and smear a bit of blusher on.

WOMAN 2: *(Weakly.)* And mentally?

WOMAN 1: *(Softens.)* I think of my husband. *(Pauses.)* He was a wonderful dancer. And so handsome. All the girls were jealous of me. *(Pause.)* That was a lifetime ago. *(Lost in another life.)*

WOMAN 2: You'll see him again one day.

WOMAN 1: I won't. He died years ago. When they came to our village. They ripped his beard. Made him dance and shot at his feet. Beat him and beat him. And the villagers stood by and said nothing.

Turned and walked away as he lay in the square bleeding… *(Pause.)* But I keep him here. With me.

The women turn and lie down to sleep. Lights change.

WOMAN 2: *(Narrates.)* The Porajmos – the genocide of the Roma-Sinti 'gypsies' across Europe – saw up to half a million 'gypsies' murdered in the same period as the Holocaust. *(Pause.)* A true mensch, the kind gypsy woman died that night. *(Pause.)* I took her shoes.

Lights change to the men's camp. The elder **MAN 1** *is in much pain and bandaging his foot with a piece of filthy rag while the younger* **MAN 2** *sits in despair. Both clearly starving and physically exhausted.*

MAN 1: I heard a rumour that there are plans to destroy one of the gas chambers, or perhaps the Allies will bomb them, but who knows?

MAN 2: *(Wearily.)* Who cares? We'll all be ashes by then anyway.

MAN 1: Where are you from, friend?

MAN 2: *(Pause.)* Theresienstadt.

MAN 1: Nobody is from Theresienstadt friend. Everyone who ended up in that wretched place had a life before. *(Pause.)* Where are you from?

MAN 2: *(Pause, shaking his head.)* I don't know, but I know where I'm going next.

MAN 1: And where will that be my friend?

MAN 2: *(Snorts in sarcastic laughter.)* Gehenna!!! Ha!

MAN 1 *tuts disapprovingly.*

MAN 2: You don't think we've done something dreadful to end up in this… this… hell?

MAN 1 *thinks reflectively. A pause.* **MAN 2** *looks at him as* **MAN 1** *continues bandaging.*

MAN 1: *(In explanation, simply.)* Frostbite.

MAN 2: We'll get our revenge if we ever get out of this g-dforsaken place.

MAN 1: I don't need revenge. *(A pause. He takes a moment.)* Surely you do not think that the Lord has forsaken us?

MAN 2: Oy gevalt! *(With as much energy as he can muster.)* G-d is dead!

MAN 1: *(Plays with his piece of bread – his food for the day that he has not yet eaten.)* Let me tell you a story my friend: A young housewife living in the town of Chelm had a very strange occurance. One morning, after buttering a piece of bread she accidentally dropped it on the floor. To her amazement, it fell butter side up. As everyone knows, whenever a buttered piece of bread is dropped on the floor, it always falls butter side down; it is a law of physics. But on this occasion it had fallen butter side up, and this was a great mystery which had to be solved. So all the Rabbis and elders and wise men of Chelm were summoned together and they spent three days in the synagogue fasting and praying and debating this unheard of event among themselves. After those three days they returned to the young housewife with this answer; "Madam, the problem is that you have buttered the wrong side of the bread."

A silence. **MAN 1** *passes* **MAN 2** *his piece of bread.* **MAN 2** *looks confused, but takes the bread, staring at it in disbelief. Hungrily eats the bread whilst shaking his head.*

SUSAN: That time was an important… eh… eh… phase in my life, in the camp – the camaraderie. It didn't last and I don't remember their names. But it was important. Very important. We wanted to survive. Somehow make it to a new world that would allow us to… to live. Of course, by then we knew about the gas chambers – death was all around us. Some tried to escape. Many others died by *(Clears throat.)* touching the electrified fence. Some people say, 'where was God?' I say, where were people?

Section 11

MALA AND EDEK

SUSAN: We heard many stories.

MALA: Edek, a Pole, had remarkably survived over four years at Auschwitz Birkenau when he was hanged following an audacious escape attempt in June of 1944. He had survived working as a mechanic. Edek –

EDEK: Number 531.

MALA: – was approximately twenty-one when he died. I loved him very much.

EDEK: Mala's external beauty was matched only with her striking spirit and refusal to be beaten. She was well known and well liked. Speaking several different languages afforded her a job as a messenger and translator which gave her freedom to move around the camp. She was twenty-six years old.

MALA: Number 19880.

EDEK: She had a generous heart and frequently kept others alive, smuggling food and doing all she could at great personal risk. I loved her very much.

MALA & EDEK: *(In unison.)* I loved him / her very much.

RABBI: The audacious escape had been planned differently by the men but Edek refused to leave without his beloved Mala.

EDEK: I will not leave without my Mala.

Echoes of Cielito Lindo in the background.

RABBI: Fearful that she would not pass as Polish, but would have distinctly 'Jewish' looks, making the escapees too noticeable on the outside, a chalk picture was drawn of Mala for the men to see. Later the plan evolved, and Mala and Edek escaped separately to the other men. Disguised in an SS uniform, Edek led a disguised Mala dressed as a male worker out of Birkenau. And so to freedom. It was June 1944.

Captured at the Slovakian border some two weeks later, Mala and Edek were returned to Auschwitz and their fates were sealed. Interrogated and tortured separately in the notorious Block 11, neither Mala nor Edek ever gave any names or information. Eventually, on 15th September, they were transferred back to Birkenau for their simultaneous executions. But the story did not end there. And resistance is possible even in death.

MALA: My beloved Edek kicked the stool from underneath himself before they could do it to him, shouting "Long Live Poland!" before the noose tightened around his neck.

EDEK: My beloved Mala would not give them the last laugh. As ever, the inmates were forced to watch as she was taken to the gallows and rather than die on their terms, she slit her wrists. There are differing stories of how she died after that. But however it was, she remained unbowed by camp life.

RABBI: May their memories be a blessing. *(Places stones beneath the tree.)* And then there was the story of Father Maximilian Kolbe. But that is another story for another time.

Section 12

TO BELSEN

SUSAN: On one occasion I was selected. I thought that was it. I just followed the mass of girls – neglected and malnourished. But we hadn't been selected for the gas chamber, but for slave labour. We were put on a train to Guben, a big industrial town, and I ended up testing some primitive electronic work… you know… did it light up? I was told what to do and… just copied. The quality and quantity of food improved so we could work better.

Music. Physicalised slave labour sequence – time passing.

SUSAN: As the Allied forces came closer, we were sent on a death march in the mid-winter. We walked and walked and walked. Across fields… you know, frozen fields and rotted roads. Hundreds of miles. If we were lucky, we slept in barns and got some boiled potatoes, or scraped for frozen food in the fields and continued walking. Those who faltered were left. I don't know if they were shot.

We walked into this death… this place of death. Bergen – Belsen. The big gates opened. I crawled in. I couldn't walk anymore. There were dead people all… on the ground… on the frozen ground. There was no distribution of food at all… People were just dying. It was unbelievable.

Auschwitz was kept clean from death because they had the gas chambers… but here… there was no hygiene whatsoever. Infectious diseases were raging… typhus and malnutrition. I had tuberculosis and many other problems. I had to get out from the barrack where I was placed because it was intolerable… corpses all over the place. I crawled into the next barrack. Remarkable, but who do I see… the first time somebody I knew from home… this woman, whose child was taken away at the railroad. Mrs Schwartz. She recognised me, and called out:

MRS SCHWARTZ: Zsuzy.

SUSAN: Well! It was just like coming alive. "Mrs Schwartz!"

MRS SCHWARTZ: What's happening to us Zsuzy? Do you think we will go on? Will we live?

SUSAN: I don't know how I found the… the sense to say: "Just hold on a bit longer Mrs Schwartz. We will make it… just hold on." I… I crawled back later to see her again… and she had all… lice on her forehead… indicating that she was dead… see… the lice feed on the blood.

Stones set by actors beneath the tree.

And then came word that the Allies were coming and the Nazis began to flee. The Nazis wanted to eradicate any signs of evil… any evidence.

NAZI: Every scrap of evidence will be destroyed. If there are survivors, no one will believe you.

SUSAN: Some victims managed to open the food storerooms. Many died after because they were unable to digest food… this type of food… um… is not recommended for those who had been under starvation for so long.

SUSAN: Bergen-Belsen, was liberated on 15th April. It wasn't a joyous day. I didn't know what joy was anymore. I crawled out… I was dying but I wanted to die outside.

The British liberators organised the rescue mission marvellously well. It's a big place Belsen and they only had small ambulances. Whenever they saw movement in a corpse, they picked it up. That's how they picked me up. They converted the German officers' barrack into a hospital. They called the local population in to say –

BRITISH SOLDIER: Look at what your Führer has done. Look at this scene of devastation.

SUSAN: I had a picture taken in the hospital, when I was rescued but tore it up. I didn't want to be reminded. Of course, one is reminded in your mind. I was severely malnourished, suffered from tuberculosis and from oedema in my leg… I've still got that… and… you know mental… mental problems.

I remember somebody saying in German, "Do you want to go to Sweden?" I had no idea where Sweden was, but I nodded. The

Swedes were very helpful in my recovery… very helpful. I wanted to go to Israel but immigration into Israel wasn't allowed. So then, I was sent to Canada and met my husband who was also a survivor. We had three children there, learnt to speak English with the help of television and I just… just did menial tasks, you know.

He didn't want to share his story… that was his way. He didn't speak about the atrocities that he witnessed in Mauthausen. Even worse than I have… it was a very sensitive thing for him. I mean, how do you live a life afterwards? Knowing your family is dead and have been murdered. Imagine yourself at fourteen; no family to care for you, no real support, no skills, no money, no language and no rights. What do you do? Some committed suicide because they couldn't live with uh… with the trauma.

Section 13

LACI

SUSAN: But there is a story afterwards… after survival. Human beings are resourceful, and so was I. Only the young survived – my age group. My brother had also survived. He told me he'd been sent to Treblinka or somewhere like that, where he'd worked as sonderkommando.

Kaddish sung quietly by the **RABBI** *in the background.*

BRITISH SOLDIER: Treblinka. A factory. Purpose built simply to murder Jews as efficiently as possible. From July 1942 to October 1943 as many as 925,000 men, women and children were murdered at this one extermination camp alone. Very few survived to tell their stories. Other extermination camps, constructed during 'Operation Reinhard' served a similar purpose with few living to spread the word of the atrocities they had seen and endured.

(Whispering.)

ALL: Bełżec, Sobibor, Chełmno, Majdanek.

(Repeated.)

BRITISH SOLDIER: And at every death camp, the Sonderkommando: Prisoners forced to clear and destroy in the crematoria daily the many thousands of bodies and the rest of the aftermath left behind in the wake of the Nazi's longstanding murder regime that had begun years before with the Einsatzgruppen – the rounding up and shooting of people across Europe. Millions more murdered before the death factories had even been built – possibly even conceived. Sonderkommando – inmates who themselves would then be sent to their deaths in the gas chambers.

LACI: My greatest fear was always that I'd be shovelling a body who was a member of my family, or just someone I knew.

SUSAN: But the war ended. I was liberated, and Laci finally returned to my parents' home in Hungary. The Red Cross created lists of survivors and displayed them back in the home towns.

LACI: I looked every day. Every day the names increased. One day… I found Zsusy. I got her address and wrote to her. "Susan, the Soviets stayed. Hard regime…

SUSAN & LACI: "Don't come home."

SUSAN: We all felt it; where was I to go… you know… where do I go? After that we used to correspond in letters, but I didn't see him then until I came to live here in England, in 1962.

LACI'S WIFE: He was very badly affected, psychologically… very badly affected. It was a… a very, very harsh regime,

SUSAN: The Soviets, ugh! His wife told me they'd arrested him…

LACI'S WIFE: Put him in a straightjacket and gave him electric shock treatment.

SUSAN: In 1966 I saved up money and took my three children to see him.

LACI is sat in silence. **SUSAN** *approaches as they talk.*

SUSAN: He'd married –

WIFE: A Hungarian woman, and had a daughter.

SUSAN: He… he said a few things… not much, because, because…

WIFE: The Soviets had accused him of treason so he couldn't work.

SUSAN: They ruined him. I brought him out a couple of times, hoping maybe he could be helped. I got him a visa to come here, as a visitor.

She moves away from him and looks hopefully at him. He remains in the chair in silence.

SUSAN: His wife then got in touch with me.

WIFE: He can't come.

SUSAN: Why?

WIFE: He's been put into a mental asylum.

SUSAN: I have to rescue him. I flew out and brought him out in the 1970s, but he just wanted to go back, of course, 'cause that's where his wife was.

WIFE: He died in 1995.

Section 14

BEING HUMAN

Avinu Malkeinu in the background.

SUSAN: I haven't lost my faith. I like my religion. I need to know that there is something more than just people here. There's always a little fear within me, that sometimes… you know… under certain conditions, people can turn into such violent beasts.

I kept in touch with one of my liberators from Belsen and said, "You were battle – worn, you were tired, and yet you had the patience and goodness to stop and help us wretches. What put that goodness in your heart? You are the real hero in my life."

I loved him to pieces, but he died, poor kid. *(Susan sets stone beneath the tree, reflecting.)*

RABBI: The ancient Hebrew word for G-d's spirit is Ruach. In the Tanakh, the word Ruach generally means wind, breath, mind and spirit. As a bird can struggle to fight against the wind, and as Mala Zimetbaum knew only too well, never losing sight of our humanity against a backdrop of atrocity, we battle with the complex knowledge of what it means to be human. *(To prayer.)*

SUSAN: Kindness still disarms me. Kindness, compassion, generosity. It is the force of life. For me, kindness is the legacy of the Holocaust.

'The Tree of Life' plays in the background as the lights fade down.

Timeline As Detailed In The Script

1930: Susan is born

1933: Hitler comes to power in Germany

1935: Reference to the family owning a telephone in their ordinary life at home

1939: Hungarian Government impose anti-Jewish legislation and Laci is beaten up

EARLY 1940S: German enforced anti-Jewish legislations begin in Hungary

JULY '42-OCT '43: The mass murders at Treblinka are carried out

1943: Susan's school is closed, Mrs Schwartz' children disappear and the men from the village are taken away, including Susan's father

SHAVUOT: *(End of May 1944)* Shavuot and Susan, her mother and brother are 'resettled' in a ghetto

GHETTO: 5 days

WALK TO MINE: 2/3 hours

MINE: 3/4 days

WALK TO WAGON TRAIN: 'a good few hours'

WAGON: 4/6 days

JUNE 1944: Susan, her mother and brother are deported to Auschwitz and separated

JUNE 1944 Mala and Edek escape Auschwitz-Birkenau

15TH SEPT. 1944 Mala and Edek are executed

'MIDWINTER' *(THEREFORE 44/45)*: Susan is forced on a death march to Bergen-Belsen

15TH APRIL '45: Bergen-Belsen is liberated (Susan recovers in Sweden)

1947: Susan resettles in Canada, meets her husband and has children

1962: Susan and her family move to England

1966: Susan visits Laci in Hungary

1970S: Susan brings Laci to the UK, but he returns to Hungary

1995: Laci dies

Glossary

ALLIES – The allied countries of the UK, USA, Russia and France who, along with others, opposed the Axis powers of Germany, Japan, Italy and others during World War 2.

ANTISEMITISM – the hostility to, prejudice or discrimination against the Jewish people.

ATAH BECHARTONU – song from a prayer recited on Jewish holidays such as Shavuot.

AUSCHWITZ-BIRKENAU – the most complex and interrelated of the Nazi camps. Auschwitz I was a concentration camp originally established for Polish political prisoners.

Auschwitz II–Birkenau [Birch Tree] located some 2 kilometres away was a death camp/killing centre complete with four crematoria, gas chambers and ovens to systematically murder people, primarily Jews, and to burn their bodies. Some one million Jews were killed in its gas chambers and 19,00 Roma and Sinti [Gypsies], men, women and children mainly between 1942 and 1944.

Auschwitz II–Buna-Monowitz was a series of industrial slave labour camps, in which German corporations invested heavily in the industrial installation believing that slavery would be a permanent part of the Nazi German economy.

AVINU MALKEINU – *(Hebrew: 'Our Father, Our King')* A prayer recited or sung at Rosh Hashanah and Yom Kippur asking for God's compassion, originally for times of great human need.

BEŁŻEC – The first of the 'Operation Reinhard' killing centres in occupied Poland. Under the leadership of Christian Wirth, who had previously worked on the T4 'euthanasia' programme to murder disabled adults and children in Germany, Belzec developed the scaling up of the gas vans of aktion T4 and Chełmno to gas chambers and the 'efficiency through deception' that marked the industrialisation of the Nazi death camps. Some 500,000 Jews were murdered at Belzec during the 10 months of its operation from March-December 1942. There were only two known survivors.

BERGEN-BELSEN – A Nazi concentration camp in north Germany. Initially a prisoner of war camp. Many thousands of prisoners brought to Bergen-Belsen from other camps across Europe died of the overcrowding, lack of food and unsanitary conditions even after the liberation of the camp in 1945. The camp, designed to hold no more than 10,000 prisoners was holding over 60,000 when liberated by the British with an additional approximately 13,000 unburied corpses lying unburied around the camp.

BUDAPEST – The capital city of Hungary. There are a number of Holocaust memorials in Budapest including that of the 'Shoes on the Danube Bank' – a powerful memorial honouring the thousands of Jews driven to the banks of the river and ordered to take off their shoes before being shot into the waters of the Danube in 1944-5.

CAMPS – A complicated variety of camps *(some 44,000)* were created by Nazi Germany and its allies between 1933 and 1945. Amongst others, there were;

– internment/concentration camps which were created for the detention of perceived enemies of the Reich,

– forced labour camps for the use of prisoners to work for the regime's economic gain through slave labour,

– transit camps for the temporary holding of Jews before deportment to killing centres,

– killing centres *('death camps')* established primarily or exclusively for the methodical mass murder of victims immediately on arrival.

Some camps such as Auschwitz-Birkenau grew to accommodate a variety of these functions.

CHALLAH – A traditional plaited bread, typically eaten on the Sabbath and many Jewish holidays.

CHELM – A fictional town of many traditional Yiddish tales in which fools, in attempts to behave wisely, act to comic effect; "Which is more important, the sun or the moon?" a citizen of Chelm asked the rabbi. "What a silly question!" snapped the cleric. "The moon, of course! It shines at night when we really need it. But who needs the sun to shine when it is already broad daylight?"

CHEŁMNO – A killing centre in occupied Poland responsible for the murder of at least 175,000 people including residents of the Łódź ghetto, between 1941 and 1945. Those deported were murdered in large gas vans and their bodies buried *(and later exhumed and burnt)* in the nearby forest. The first stationary facility where poison gas was used to murder Jews.

CIELITO LINDO – *(trans. 'Lovely sweet one')* A song from Mexico popularised in 1882. The melody was re-purposed with new lyrics by the resistance movement in Poland during occupation by the Nazis.

'COFFEE' – Boiled water, generally with some grain based coffee / tea substitute added.

CZÁRDÁS – A traditional Hungarian folk dance.

DR MENGELE – *(Josef Mengele)* An SS physician who used Nazi racial theories to justify conducting inhumane experiments on prisoners at Auschwitz from 1943, causing horrific injuries and death to many children and families. He is documented as often appearing 'off duty' at the selection area for new arrivals searching for twins to conduct experiments on. Mengele evaded justice, fleeing to Argentina and died in Brazil in 1979.

EDEK GALINSKI – Edward 'Edek' Galinski was amongst the first Polish political prisoners sent to Auschwitz. He had fought in the Polish army and was arrested in Spring 1940 during an operation against the Polish resistance. He survived four years working in the camp, falling in love with inmate Mala Zimetbaum during this time. Following a successful escape, they were recaptured and executed after a period of interrogation and torture during which neither betrayed any of their co-conspirators.

EINSATZGRUPPEN – Special task forces, often referred to as 'mobile killing squads' who followed the German army as it invaded countries in north-eastern Europe. Often working with local collaborators, they committed mass shootings of Jews as well as political enemies and other civilians. Up to one third of all Holocaust victims were killed in these actions that preceeded the death camps of Operation Reinhard.

EICHMANN – *(Adolf Eichmann)* SS Obersturmbannfuhrer Eichmann was one of the key organisers of the Holocaust. Eichmann was captured in 1960, tried and hanged in Israel in 1962. While awaiting trial he famously stated: "to sum it all up, I must say that I regret nothing" (*LIFE magazine, 1960*). In describing Eichmann, Hannah Arendt coined the term 'the banality of evil'.

FASCIST – Fascism, in simple terms, is a far right ultranationalistic dictatorship putting the nation *(and often race)* and the economy above the individual.

FATHER MAXIMILIAN KOLBE – A Franciscan monk from Poland. Kolbe supervised a friary near Warsaw from 1936 where, after German invasion, the friars sheltered some 3,000 refugees including 2,000 Jews. In 1939 the Friary was closed and Kolbe was amongst those sent to Auschwitz where he continued his good work. In 1941, when ten men were selected for death by starvation to punish the inmates for another's escape, one of the selected men cried out in pain that he wanted to live for his wife and children. In an act of characteristic selflessness, Kolbe volunteered to take his place. After two weeks without food or water, to clear the cell for other inmates, Kolbe was killed by lethal injection. He was canonised by Pope John Paul II in 1982.

GAS CHAMBER – A sealed chamber for killing with gas *(eg. Hydrogen cyanide, carbon dioxide, carbon monoxide)* introduced to the space. In the USA, small chambers were used for executing condemned prisoners from the 1920s and were used similarly by a number of other countries. From 1939, during the Nazi regime gas vans and improvised chambers were used as part of the T4 'euthanasia' programmes in Germany and beyond. These were further extended and developed as an efficient methodology for murder, culminating in the industrialised factories of Operation Reinhard (see below) that initially used carbon monoxide and then hydrogen cyanide *(a pesticide, brand name – Zyklon B)* at Auschwitz-Birkenau killing up to 6,000 a day.

GEFILTE FISH – A ground fish dish, traditionally served as a first course on the Sabbath, Passover and other holidays in Ashkenazi communities.

GEHENNA – 'The Valley of the Damned' in the afterlife; named after a valley south west of Jerusalem where kings of Judah sacrificed their children by fire. An accursed place of torment and misery.

GENDARMES – The forces responsible for policing the Hungarian countrysides. From 1941, they were involved in the roundups of Jews during the Einsatzgruppen murders and from 1944, during German occupation, the round ups for ghettoisation and deportation to killing centres. Their cruelty and barbarity is documented as shocking even some of the Nazi occupiers.

GHETTO – A place created for the segregation of a group of people away from the rest of a community. Originally the term was used for the area in Venice *(Italy)* in the 16th century where Jews were forced to live in poverty away from the rest of the population.

G-D – A sign of reverence when writing the name of the creator that is considered holy. To not write the name in full is to prevent the possibility of destruction or disposing of the Lord's name.

GUBEN – *(Gubin)* An industrialised town on the Polish – German border where factories used slave labour for munitions and other work for the German war effort.

HEBREW – The language of the Jewish bible *(the Tanakh)*, of prayer and the official language of modern Israel.

HINE MA TOV – A hymn sung traditionally at Sabbath. The lyrics begin "how good and how pleasant for people to sit together in unity".

HOLOCAUST – The deliberate attempt by the Nazi regime to systematically annihilate the entire Jewish population during WW2. From the Greek word meaning 'sacrifice by fire' the term is problematic given the nature of the destruction of the six million *(approximately)* Jews murdered and therefore the term 'Shoah' (Hebrew for 'catastrophe') is preferred by many. Whilst it is acknowledged, importantly, to also recognise that many other victims were targeted for persecution and murder by the regime *(see, for example 'Porajmos')*, the Holocaust is a specific term for the genocide of the Jewish people during World War Two.

KADDISH – *(sanctification)* Often used to refer to 'The Mourner's Kaddish'; a prayer in Aramaic as part of the ritual of mourning for the dead, including at a funeral and memorial.

KAPO – A concentration camp prisoner forced to oversee other prisoners, usually on labour detail.

KOSHER – Food that complies to the Jewish laws of Kashrut; religious tradition.

LATKES – Shallow fried potato pancakes.

ŁÓDŹ – The third largest city in occupied Poland and home to nearly one third of the Jewish population of Poland. The Łódź ghetto suffered from similarly horrific living conditions to other ghettos before its inhabitants were sent to death camps. Its Jewish leader, Mordechai Chaim Rumkowski's leadership differed markedly to the leadership, for example, of Adam Czerniaków in the Warsaw ghetto who ultimately committed suicide when he realised his attempts to save the Jews under his leadership had failed when the deportations to Treblinka began.

LOKSHEN KUGEL – An Ashkenazi dish usually served at Shabbat and Yom Tov. Sweet egg noodle *(lokshen)* based baked pudding *(kugel)* usually with milk / cottage cheese and raisins.

MALA ZIMETBAUM – The first woman to escape from Auschwitz-Birkenau, Mala was a Belgian Jewish translator at the camp having previously been a brilliant student of several European languages before being forced out of education due to her family's poverty. Having fallen in love with Edek Galinski at Auschwitz they escaped together but were recaptured at the Slovakian border, sent back to Auschwitz, tortured and then executed after refusing to name co-conspirators. Mala and Edek both took their own lives at the gallows as a final act of resistance.

MATZAH – An unleavened bread traditionally baked for Passover, usually served as flat cracker like bread, or as breadcrumbs and in traditional matzah ball soup. It symbolises the exodus from Egypt when, in the rush to flee, there was no time for the bread *(that was being baked for provisions)* to rise. It symbolises both freedom and the importance to remain humble in the memory of one's history.

MAJDANEK – Primarily a transit and labour camp with brutal conditions that saw tens of thousands die in horrific slave conditions – initially Soviet prisoners of war and then Jews deported from all over Poland and beyond. From the winter of 1941 Majdanek also developed three gas chambers to directly murder Jews in addition to those thousands dying from starvation, disease, freezing conditions and physical abuse. Made nervous by Jewish armed resistance movements in other cities and camps, in November 1943 additional SS were dispatched to Majdanek for Operation 'Harvest Festival'. Some 18,000 victims were shot at the site, with music playing on loudspeakers throughout to drown out the sound of the massacre; the largest single day single location killing during the Holocaust.

MAUTHAUSEN – Nicknamed 'the bone grinder', this was one of the most brutal camps of the Nazi concentration / labour camps and was largely intended to murder – primarily through tortuous labour – the intelligentsia, political prisoners and 'higher' social classes of the societies subjugated by the Nazi regime. Prisoners were forced into hard labour at the granite quarries, the mining of which supported the reconstruction of German towns and the Nazi architectural plans of Albert Speer.

MENSCH – *(Yiddish)* A person of exceptional integrity and honour; who acts with restraint, humility and compassion.

OEDEMA – A painful condition commonly found in survivors of the camps at liberation; caused by fluid built up in the feet and ankles or lungs, often leading to heart or respiratory failure.

OPERATION REINHARD – The code-name for the planned extermination of the Jews in German occupied Europe. It was planned in 1941 but so titled by the Nazi leadership after the murder of Reinhard Heydrich by Czech resistance fighters in 1942. The death camps *(or killing centres)* of Belzec, Sobibor and Treblinka as well as Chelmno, Auschwitz II and Majdanek were established or developed as part of this aktion. The killing centres *(so called 'death camps')* of Belzec, Sobibor and Treblinka which constituted Aktion Reinhard were established in the winter, spring and summer of 1942.

OY VEY – *(Yiddish)* An exclamation of dismay.

OY GEVALT! – *(Yiddish)* An exclamation of dismay or exasperation.

PORAJMOS – *(Romani – 'the devouring')* The attempted genocide of the Romani population of occupied Europe. The Roma – Sinti people *(often called 'gypsies')* were another group considered 'racially inferior' by the Nazis. Exact figures cannot be ascertained but it is estimated that up to 250,000 of a population of approximately one million in Europe were murdered during the regime.

PROPAGANDA – Misleading information created to promote a point of view or political cause, generally using language and imagery with bias to create an emotional rather than objective response in order to affect mass behaviour. Julius Streicher, for example, was an author of Nazi propaganda literature including *Der Sturmer* and various books for children *(and a multimillionaire as a result of his work)*. He was convicted of crimes against humanity at the Nuremberg trials and hanged for his part in the Holocaust which acknowledged the power and impact of propaganda in its role in the atrocities of the Nazi regime.

RABBI – A spiritual or religious leader in Judaism.

REINHARD HEYDRICH – A trusted member of Hitler's inner circle. In charge of the Gestapo and SD during the 30s, and then as Reich Protector of Bohemia and Moravia from 1941, Heydrich was tasked with leadership of the 'solution to the Jewish Question', the Einsatzgruppen from 1939 and, after the Wansee conference in 1942, the killing centres in Poland – 'the final solution'. He died after an assassination attempt by Czech resistance fighters in 1943. Subsequently, the murder regime at the death camps was re-named 'Operation Reinhard' in his 'honour' *(see above)*.

'RESETTLEMENT' – One of many euphemisms used by the Nazis. 'Resettlement in the East', as 'euthanasia' was used to describe murder. In the case of 'resettlement', this was generally at one of the killing centres established in occupied Poland.

ROLL CALL – Inmates in the camp would be forced to stand in rows, often for several hours and in all weathers, to be counted. Generally, but not exclusively, morning and night – before and after labour. The dead would also be lined up and in the case of error, counting would be restarted, extending the torment even further. Roll calls often included witnessing punishments and executions to further contain any possible desire amongst prisoners for resistance or rebellion as well as to further the degradation and dehumanisation of the inmates.

ROMA / SINTI – 'Gypsy' is generally a pejorative term used to describe Roma and Sinti people who were considered 'asocial' and 'racially inferior' by the Nazi regime. Romani derive from a nomadic people who migrated from northern India to Europe. In 1935, in a supplementary decree to the Nuremberg Laws, Romani were classified as 'enemies of the race based state' placing them in the same category as the Jews and therefore condemning them to a fate in some ways similar to the Jews in the Holocaust *(see Porajmos)*.

RUACH – In Kabbalah, 'Ruach' is considered a higher plane of consciousness than 'Nefesh' – the life force of the body given by G-d. It is considered entwined with human emotions, particularly of love and compassion as well as awe in G-d's divine energy. In the Talmud, the sages refer to it as 'the toil of the heart, through which one finds love'.

SHABBAT – *(Sabbath)* The Jewish holy day. From the Hebrew 'Shabbat' *(to rest)*. The Sabbath begins at sunset on Friday and lasts until sunset on Saturday. It is marked with the lighting of the Shabbat candles, with traditional meals and prayer. It is a spiritual time and a day of rest to spend time with family.

SELECTION – The process of 'selection' happened at camps where those deported, if deemed fit for slave labour, would be separated from those sent to their death. Selections of those kept in camps to work would take place regularly with SS doctors and wardens separating those no longer deemed 'useful' due to the continually incoming deportations which created an ongoing 'supply' of slaves for the labour force.

SHALOM – *(Hebrew)* Generally translated as 'peace'. Used as both 'hello' and 'goodbye' as a greeting.

SHAVUOT – A major Jewish festival that commemorates the giving of the Torah *(Jewish laws)* on Mount Sinai and linked to the festival of Passover. Customarily, dairy foods are eaten as the first meal of Shavuot and meat meals to be eaten separately afterwards.

SOBIBOR – Constructed in spring 1942 as the second killing centre of 'Operation Reinhard' in the east of occupied Poland and initially led by SS Commandant Franz Stangl *(experienced in the T4 programme)*. As in other death camps, Sonderkommandos *(see below)* were forced to process the estimated 170,000 – 270,000 bodies of people murdered in the gas chambers there, burying them in mass graves as well as processing their belongings. In October 1943, the sonderkommando staged an uprising, with some 300 prisoners escaping. Nearly sixty escapees survived until the end of the war. Within days of the uprising, Himmler ordered the camp to be dismantled.

SONDERKOMMANDO – *(German – 'special command unit')* Groups of Jewish prisoners kept alive as forced labour largely, but not exclusively to deal with and dispose of those murdered in the killing centres. Groups were forced to sort hidden valuables, remove gold teeth, shave bodies and bury or burn the corpses of those murdered. Used in order to maximise efficiency and minimise the impact of these traumatic tasks for SS personnel, these slave labourers were aware of their limited life spans and acts of resistance are well documented; generally units were, themselves murdered after a few months to limit the witnesses to the atrocities.

'SOUP' – Prisoners received three 'meals' a day in Auschwitz-Birkenau *(for example)*. For breakfast, a boiled water drink *(see 'coffee')*, at lunchtime a portion of 'soup' – made generally from potatoes, flour, food extracts and other basic ingredients, and at supper about 300 grams of a black coloured hard bread with perhaps a piece of sausage or margarine or a tablespoon of marmalade for example. Newly arrived inmates could often not stomach the food and the insufficient nutritional value led quickly to emaciation and starvation sickness.

SS / SCHUTZSTAFFEL – *(German – 'Protection Squad')* The paramilitary branch of the Nazi party run by Heinrich Himmler from 1925 and expanded to 250,000 members by the start of World War II. They were responsible for a wide variety of activities from intelligence operations to running the Nazi concentration and death camps. Not to be confused with the SA *(assault division / 'brown shirts')* who were Hitler's private army of stormtroopers, established in 1921 to support and perpetrate violence against Jews and political adversaries.

SYNAGOGUE – A consecrated space, used for the purpose of prayer, study and assembly of Jewish communities. Halakha states however, that Jewish worship can be carried out wherever ten Jews congregate, so synagogues are not always necessary for a Jewish community but are often a centrepoint for Jewish life.

TANAKH / TORAH / TALMUD – The Tanakh *(the Hebrew Bible)* is a collection of scriptures including the Torah *(the first five books of Moses)*. The Talmud is, essentially an interpretation of the scriptures by ancient Rabbis, providing guidance on the laws, traditions etc. of Jewish life.

THE FÜHRER – *(German – 'leader' or guide)* A title Adolf Hitler gave himself from 1934 as he rose to ultimate power in Germany. In 1933, he became the chancellor of Germany and after the death of President Von Hindenberg and a series of actions, including the Enabling Act, Hitler took both roles and named himself 'Führer', ultimately blending both roles to become a dictator in total power of Nazi Germany. One of the

Nazis' most common slogans was 'Ein Volk, Ein Reich, Ein Fuhrer' – 'One People, One Empire, One Leader'.

THERESIENSTADT – *(Terezin)* Created from the old fortress town of Terezin in Bohemia and Moravia after German occupation, Theresienstadt fulfilled a number of roles; as a transit camp for Czech Jews to be deported to concentration, forced labour and death camps, as a labour camp that also concealed the mass murder of the Jews. Significant figures from cultural life in various countries were deported there in order to function as a propaganda machine and, famously, for a visit from the International Red Cross in 1944 to prove that treatment of those deported was 'good'. Conditions, in reality, were so horrendous that tens of thousands died there and a crematorium was constructed to the south of the ghetto in 1942. The clandestine nature of the work of artists, writers, musicians, actors and politicians imprisoned there is noteworthy, including their efforts to sustain the children sent there through the arts and education.

TREBLINKA – Treblinka I served as a forced labour camp, whilst Treblinka II, established as part of 'Operation Reinhard', was a killing centre that took the lives of an estimated 1 million people. Over 900,000 of these were Jewish, including more than ½ million from the Warsaw ghetto. The gas chambers ran on carbon monoxide fumes, as Sobibor did, and bodies were buried and later exhumed to be burnt in huge trenches. To disguise its true role as an extermination site, it was furnished with fake train schedules, a train station clock and fake ticket booth in order to help keep those sent there compliant on the way to their deaths. Much like the other death camps, there were revolts at Treblinka by the Sonderkommando with some 300 prisoners escaping in August 1943. The camp was dismantled shortly thereafter.

TUBERCULOSIS – A bacterial infection that mainly affects the lungs, but can spread to glands, bones, nervous system. Outbreaks in the camps were common and generally fatal due to starvation and subsequently weakened immune systems as well as the lack of medical care.

TYPHUS – An infectious disease spread commonly by lice in densely populated, unsanitary conditions leading to fever, rash, infection or inflammation of the brain and generally, when untreated, death.

VAC – A town in Hungary north of Budapest, on the bank of the river Danube.

YIDDISH – The language used by many Ashkenazi Jews *(primarily in Eastern European countries)* before the Holocaust. A largely Germanic dialect with vocabulary and rhythms from Hebrew as well as Slavic languages. With the post Holocaust diaspora, and with the establishment of Israel, there was a thrust amongst the surviving Jews to return to Hebrew *(albeit a modernised version)* as their origin, semitic, language.

Phonetic Pronunciations

Auschwitz-Birkenau – Owshvits-Birkenow

Belzec – Belzets

Budapest – Boodapesht

Challah – Hhalah

Chelm – Hhelm

Chelmno – Hhelmno

Czárdás – Chardash

Mengele – Men geh leh

Edek Galinski – Edeck Galinskey

Einsatzgruppen – Einsatsgroupen *(Ein as in 'mine')*

Eichmann – Ickeman *(Eich as in 'hike')*

Maximilian Kolbe – Maximilian Kolbeh

Felsögod – Felshogood

Führer- Fewruh

Gefilte fish – Gerfilter fish

Gehenna – Gehenna *(G as in 'get')*

Gendarmes – Shondarms

Guben – Gooben

Kapos – Cappoes

Kosher – Koasher *(as in 'coat')*

Laci – Lotsy

Lodz – Woodge

Lokshen kugel – Lockshen koogel

Matzah – Mutsuh

Majdanek – Mazhdenek/Mydarnik

Mauthausen – Mouthouwsen

Mensch – Mench

Oedema – Uhdeemah/Edeemah

Porajmos – Poriymos

Reinhard Heydrich – Rinehard Highdrish

Ruach – Rooak

Schwartz – Shwarts/Shvarts

Shavuot – Shavuort

Sobibor – Sobeebor

Sonderkommando – Sonderkomarndoh

Theresienstadt *(Terezin)* – Tereesienshtat *(Terezin)*

Treblinka – Treblinker

Vac – Vack

Wie alt bist du – Vee ult bist do

Zsuzsanna / Zsuzy – Shoesharner/Shoeshe

Omsk, Tomsk, Irkutsk, Vladivostok – Oomsk, Toomsk, Earkoosk, Vladeevostock

Key Organisations / Research Resources

Auschwitz-Birkenau Memorial and Museum

http://auschwitz.org/en/

Echoes and Reflections

echoesandreflections.org

HET (Holocaust Educational Trust)

het.org.uk

HMDT (Holocaust Memorial Day Trust)

hmd.org.uk

Holocaust Theatre International Initiative

htc.miami.edu/about-holocaust-theater-archive/

IHRA (International Holocaust Remembrance Alliance)

holocaustremembrance.com/world-remembers-holocaust

IWM (Imperial War Museum)

iwm.org.uk/

Jewish Partisans Educational Foundation

https://www.jewishpartisans.org/what-is-a-jewish-partisan

National Holocaust Centre and Museum (UK)

holocaust.org.uk/

UCL Centre for Holocaust Education

holocausteducation.org.uk/

USC Shoah Foundation

sfi.usc.edu/

USHMM (United States Holocaust Memorial Museum)

https://www.ushmm.org/

Voices of the Holocaust (Holocaust Theatre in Education)

voicesoftheholocaust.org.uk

Salamander Street

Teachers – if you are interested in buying a set of texts for your class please email info@salamanderstreet.com – we would be happy to discuss discounts and keep you up to date with our latest publications and study guides.

Printed in the USA
CPSIA information can be obtained
at www.ICGtesting.com
JSHW051959150824
68134JS00057B/3480